D1418667

BEAUTIFUL SHEEP

JOURNAL

Ivy Press

A SHEEP SPOTTER'S FIELD GUIDE

BORDER LEICESTER

Where seen..

Date..

Notes...

COTSWOLD

Where seen..

Date..

Notes...

HERDWICK

Where seen..

Date..

Notes...

SHETLAND

Where seen..

Date..

Notes...

SUFFOLK

Where seen..

Date..

Notes...

GREYFACE DARTMOOR

Where seen..

Date..

Notes...

JACOB

Where seen..

Date..

Notes...

WENSLEYDALE

Where seen..

Date..

Notes...

GALWAY

Where seen...

Date...

Notes...

 BRITISH BLEU DU MAINE

Where seen...

Date...

Notes...

 **PORTLAND**

Where seen...

Date...

Notes...

 SOUTHDOWN

Where seen...

Date...

Notes...

EXMOOR HORN

Where seen...

Date...

Notes...

 HILL RADNOR

Where seen...

Date...

Notes...

 KERRY HILL

Where seen...

Date...

Notes...

 **BLACK WELSH MOUNTAIN**

Where seen...

Date...

Notes...

BORDER LEICESTER
EWE YEARLING

Classified as a longwool breed, the BORDER LEICESTER was originally bred in the north of England. It now has a large worldwide population and is said to have been introduced to the USA by George Washington, who kept a small purebred flock at his Mount Vernon estate on the Potomac River.

COTSWOLD
RAM SHEARLING

The Cotswold is one of the ancient breeds of England, and it helped to shape the economic history of the country. Despite this, the breed was coming near to extinction at the beginning of the twentieth century, but has now regained popularity and grown in numbers across the world.

HERDWICK
EWE YEARLING

Herdwick sheep are probably the most hardy of all the UK's breeds of hill sheep, grazing in the mountainous dales of the English Lake District, which has fells rising to more than 915 m (3,000 ft) above sea level. The word 'herdwyck', meaning sheep pasture, is recorded in documents as far back as the twelfth century.

SHETLAND
RAM

The SHETLAND is one of the oldest Scottish breeds, dating back to the late eighth century, when it is believed to have been introduced to the Shetland Isles by the Vikings. Although in serious decline by the 1980s, after eleven years in the care of the Rare Breeds Survival Trust it is no longer classified as rare.

SUFFOLK
EWE YEARLING

The Suffolk was first recognized as a pure breed in 1810. Suffolks were exported from the late nineteenth century and are widely distributed in most of the principal sheep-producing countries throughout the world. They are by far the most popular purebred sheep in the USA; they are also the leading terminal sire breed in the UK.

GREYFACE DARTMOOR
EWE SHEARLING

This longwool breed from the West Country moors of England has a distinctive fleece of long and curly wool, classified as Lustre Longwool. Also known as the Improved Dartmoor, the GREYFACE DARTMOOR is an extremely hardy breed, developed to withstand the severe winters of the high moorland around Dartmoor.

JACOB
RAM LAMB

The Jacob is a very ancient breed of sheep originating in the Middle East. Importation of Jacobs to the USA and Canada has occurred in small numbers since the early 1900s, and in the UK ewes are included in the commercial flock because of the breed's hardiness, ease of lambing and strong mothering instincts.

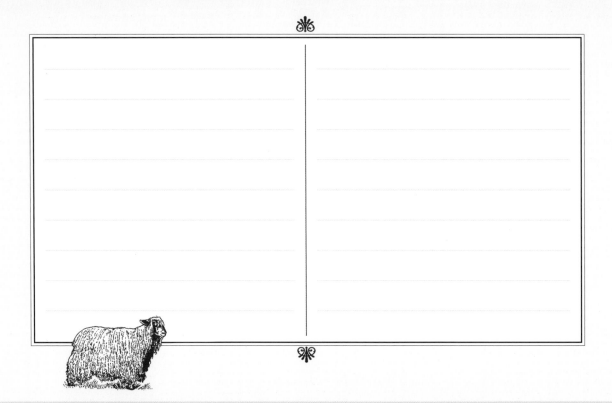

WENSLEYDALE
EWE

The WENSLEYDALE is one of the most distinctive longwool breeds, with its commanding body size and presence. Most Wensleydales have white wool, though some have black. The Wensleydale's fleece falls in long ringlets, almost to ground level, and contains no kemp (the coarse fibre present in wool). The wool is of high quality and valuable lustre.

GALWAY
RAM

Known from the eighteenth century as the Roscommon, after the Irish Lord Roscommon, the GALWAY, as it was renamed in the twentieth century, developed in western Ireland after the importation of English Leicester breeds. The Galway is currently on the Rare Breeds Survival Trust's Priority List in the UK.

PORTLAND
RAM

The PORTLAND is a heathland sheep, which has been found in its native Dorset area of south-west England for many hundreds of years. It is a member of the tan-faced group of breeds. Despite rescue from near-extinction in the 1920s, the Portland is still classified by the Rare Breeds Survival Trust as being at risk.

EXMOOR HORN
EWE YEARLING

The Exmoor Horn sheep of today are direct descendants of the horned sheep that roamed the hills of Exmoor, in England, for centuries. Like the Exmoor Pony, they are a hardy breed that can withstand harsh winters and are crucial to the maintenance of the open moorland of the Exmoor National Park.

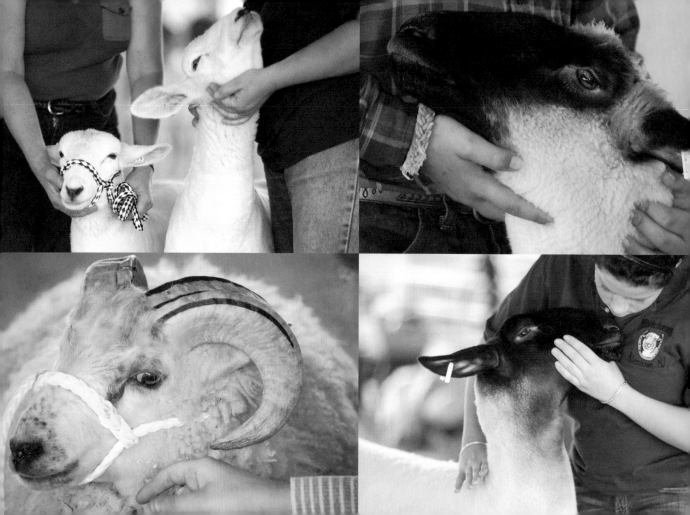

KERRY HILL
EWE YEARLING

A strikingly handsome and showy sheep with a distinctive panda face, the KERRY HILL used to be extremely numerous around the English/Welsh border, but is less popular nowadays. The breed was first exported to Holland in 1992 and is also found in Ireland. The Kerry Hill's wool is kemp-free and very soft.

BRITISH BLEU DU MAINE
EWE SHEARLING

First introduced into the UK from France in 1978, the BLEU DU MAINE has won sheep interbreed titles at both the Royal Show in England and the Royal Welsh Show. It has proven to be a very versatile animal with good carcass qualities and fine wool. The French breed developed from crossing imported Wensleydales and Leicester Longwools.

SOUTHDOWN
RAM SHEARLING

The SOUTHDOWN is an old English breed, dating back to at least the mid-1700s although its lineage stretches back much further. Extremely popular in England until the middle of the twentieth century, it has been exported across the world, with particular success in New Zealand, Australia and France.

HILL RADNOR
RAM YEARLING

The HILL RADNOR is a hill breed, most commonly found in the Welsh counties of Powys and Gwent and the surrounding areas. The breed is currently classified as 'vulnerable' by the British Rare Breeds Survival Trust. The Hill Radnor's dense fleece is popular with local weavers and hand-spinners.

BLACK WELSH MOUNTAIN
RAM YEARLING

The BLACK WELSH MOUNTAIN is a small, dual-purpose hill breed with a natural resistance to disease. The breed is prolific, hardy and self-reliant, qualities that make it ideal for both the smallholder and the larger commercial producer. Its naturally black wool doesn't need dying and is often blended with white wools.

First published in the UK in 2010 by
Ivy Press
210 High Street
Lewes
East Sussex BN7 2NS
United Kingdom
www.ivypress.co.uk

ISBN: 978-1-907332-14-2

British Library Cataloguing-in-Publication Data
A catalogue record for this book is available from
the British Library

This book was conceived, designed and produced by
Ivy Press

Printed in China

10 9 8 7 6 5 4 3 2 1